Table of Contents

What Is a Flood? **5**

River Floods **7**

Flash Floods **17**

Floods Caused by People **21**

Staying Safe **25**

More about Floods **28**

Flood Facts **29**

Further Reading **30**

Glossary **31**

Index **32**

4

What Is a Flood?

This town has been flooded. Water is everywhere! A flood is when water covers an area that is usually dry. What makes a flood happen?

This river in Gloucestershire has too much
water and is flowing over its banks.

River Floods

A river can cause a flood. Think of your bath. It can only hold so much water. If you add more, water flows over the sides. Like baths, rivers can only hold so much water. When a river gets more water than it can hold, it flows over its **banks**.

Grass and other plants take in some rainwater
that falls to the ground.

Too much rain can cause a river to
overflow. If it rains a lot, the ground
cannot soak up all the water. The extra
rainwater flows down to the river.

But the river can't hold all the extra
water. The river flows over its banks.

In snowy areas, the weather can warm up quickly in the spring. Then the snow melts fast, and turns into water.

Melted snow makes puddles on the frozen ground.

The water runs downhill into rivers.
Too much water makes rivers overflow.
Houses on the **floodplain** get flooded.

In cold areas, rivers freeze in the winter. In the spring, the ice breaks into large chunks as it melts. The chunks float down the river.

Sometimes, the chunks of ice get stuck and block the river. The river water runs over its banks.

Some rivers have **dams**. Dams can control the flow of river water. But sometimes rain brings too much water.

This large dam was built across a river in China. Floodgates let water through the dam's wall.

The rising water pushes through the
dam's wall. Water rushes over the
dam, causing a flood.

Heavy rains caused this flash flood.

Flash Floods

Flash floods happen when lots of water comes quickly. Burst dams can cause flash floods. Big storms and melting snow can also bring lots of water in a short time. A wall of water rushes downhill. It takes mud, rocks and trees with it.

Floodwater fills buildings and streets.
Cars can get stuck in the water.

Floodwater dragged this house down a river
and left it on top of a bridge.

Sometimes cars, houses and people
are swept away by the rushing water.

This flooded road was built through a **wetland**.

Floods Caused by People

Wetlands catch and store lots of water. But people sometimes drain wetlands to build on them. People pave over the land to build roads, houses or shopping centres.

But roads and pavements can't absorb water. During heavy rain, the water runs off the roads.

Heavy rains flooded this street in India.

The water flows into streets, buildings, lakes and rivers. Many towns and cities get flooded.

These scientists are lowering a tool into a river.
The tool will track the flow of the water.

Staying Safe

Scientists try to work out when and where floods will occur. They use special tools to keep track of rainfall. They also watch the flow of rivers and streams. Scientists warn people if a flood is coming.

Look out for **flood warnings** on the radio, TV or Internet. The warnings will tell you how to stay safe.

Evacuate if told to do so. If you can't leave your home, make sure you stay higher than the floodwater. Rescue workers will come to help you.

MORE ABOUT FLOODS

Preserving wetlands, river channels and floodplains helps to control flooding. People often fill in river channels. They build houses on wetlands and floodplains. Then the floodwater has nowhere to go. People who live in these areas often build dams and **dykes** to try to hold back the water. Dykes are walls along the side of a river. But dams and dykes can break and cause terrible flooding. A better solution is to protect or create wetlands *(right)* where floodwater can go. People should also build houses and roads away from floodplains.

Flood Facts

- Floods are the most common natural disaster worldwide. Around 40 per cent of natural disasters are floods.

- Floods can happen slowly, over days or weeks. Or they can happen quickly, within hours.

- Floods help some areas. Floodwater brings rich soil for farmers.

- One of the worst floods in UK history happened in June and July 2007. Heavy rain caused floods across the country. It was the wettest summer on record.

- Around two million homes have been built on floodplains in the UK.

Further Reading

Books

Baldwin, Carol. *Wild Waters: Floods* (Raintree Freestyle: Turbulent Planet) Raintree, 2005.

Chambers, Catherine. *Flood* (Wild Weather) Heinemann Library, 2008.

Clifford, Clive. *Flooding and Drought* (Looking at Landscapes) Evans Brothers Ltd., 2005.

Websites

Floodline Kids
http://www.sepa.org.uk/floodlinekids/index.html
This website is packed with useful information about floods. Find out how we can predict and prevent floods and take an 'understanding water' quiz.

Newsround – Floods
http://news.bbc.co.uk/cbbcnews/hi/newsid_6910000/newsid_6915000/6915037.stm
See some amazing pictures of the floods that hit the UK in June and July 2007. Read about how it affected people all over the country.

Glossary

banks: raised land around a river, lake or sea

dams: walls built across rivers to hold back some or all of the water

dykes: mounds of soil built along rivers. These mounds prevent water from flooding nearby land.

evacuate: to move from an area of danger to a safer place

flash floods: a flood that happens very quickly

floodplain: the flat area along the sides of a river that gets covered by water when the river overflows

flood warnings: notices by the government that tell people when and where a flood will occur

wetland: an area where water covers the soil for most of the year

Index

buildings 11, 18, 19, 21,
    23, 28

cars 18–19
causes of floods 7, 8,
    10–11, 13, 15, 17, 21

damage from floods 11,
    18–19, 23, 28
dams 14–15, 17, 28
danger from floods 18–19

flash floods 17–19
flood control 14, 28
floodplains 11, 28
flood warnings 25–27

ground 8, 10

ice 12–13

rain 8, 14, 16, 22, 23, 25
riverbanks 6, 7, 9, 13
rivers 6–9, 11, 12–13, 14,
    19, 23, 24, 25, 28
roads 18, 20, 21, 22, 23

snow 10, 17
staying safe in floods
    26–27
storms 17

tracking floods 24, 25

wetlands 20, 21, 28

First published in the United States of America in 2009
Text copyright © 2009 by Lerner Publishing Group, Inc.